Insofar

Sarah Gridley

New Issues Poetry & Prose

A Green Rose Book

New Issues Poetry & Prose
The College of Arts and Sciences
Western Michigan University
Kalamazoo, Michigan 49008

First Edition, 2020.

ISBN: 978-1-936970-65-0 (paperbound)

Library of Congress Cataloging-in-Publication Data:
Gridley, Sarah
Insofar/Sarah Gridley
Library of Congress Catalog Card Number: 2019055289

Editor:	Nancy Eimers
Managing Editor:	Kimberly Kolbe
Associate Editors:	Alyssa Jewell & Connor Yeck
Art Direction:	Nicholas Kuder
Design:	Amelia Manley
Production:	Paul Sizer
	The Design Center, Frostic School of Art
	College of Fine Arts
	Western Michigan University
Printing:	McNaughton & Gunn, Inc.

Insofar

Sarah Gridley

New Issues

WESTERN MICHIGAN UNIVERSITY

Also by Sarah Gridley

Weather Eye Open
Green is the Orator
Loom

for Jeremy Hooker

then,
for a breath,
there was no sign of us.
Not a soul, only
light flooding this field,
bright as a marigold.

Contents

Foreword

We can go this far,
this is ours, to touch one another this lightly...
—Rainer Maria Rilke

Insofar as expression has been matched to sensation and perception,
human nature has seemed to retain consciousness.
—Shirley Hazzard

What are Communication's
Mistakes in the magic medium doing
To us? It matters only in
So far as we want to be telling
Each other alive about each other
Alive.
—W.S. Graham

We may speak of eidola only as they "seem," "appear to be," or what they
"liken unto." Our statements must be prefixed by an "as," as if that little
word is the coin we offer Charon for taking us across the separating waters
between two kinds of speech. The dead speak differently: they whisper. Their
talk has lost its positive substance, its natural certainty. We must lean in close
to hear this kind of speech.
—James Hillman

Insofar

Sarah Gridley

Afterward

The workshop was the tidiest
of any we had seen in the Open Studio Walk.
It took up the top floor of an old brick warehouse.
There was a long climb up a spacious stairwell.
The only furniture were tables, long ones,
the kind you might see in a refectory, used hard,
but taken care of, arranged in a preferred
coherence. Owing to a wall of windows,
the top floor light was natural.
It shone the length of the workshop tables
and touched the glass they kept chromatically sorted.
My father and I looked at the boxes. I wonder
what he felt at the time.
Each box was filled with chunks of glass. Violet
in the violet box, yellow in the yellow,
indigo in the indigo, and so on.
It might have been mistaken for a meal,
so disciplined, and ordinary was the ambience.
The glaziers had taken a guild approach to art.
The space was inviting and ordinary. They were tending
the fire and ruin, the parts of the sky that flinch.
Here were the metallic salts
through which our solar prayers could break
or glow. Their trade was stained glass.
They had made it open
to the ticketed public. It felt,
and did not feel, contemporary.

Alibi

You may not ever get used to it, these house
and hemlock shadows, the more experienced
sunlight turning pages with the snow. The
jury would appear to believe your story.
You were killing time at the time in question,
from the mammal stalls of dusk to the iciest
sticks of evening. Ask any of the vanishing
beeches, the gray half-brothers you hadn't
known were yours.

All Earth Wears

Euonymus starts the yellowest green,
and quince flowers in May are the real taste of crimson.
So the looked-for calls you through its seasons, retracting
and lengthening its reach. Like a classics teacher
looking out a window thinking of his wife, the looked-for
could be so small, a smallness synonymous
with coinage width, peripheral as cups of childhood
rain, mislaid or imagined, given up on, or stored away,
bright in its loose change like pressed flowers
falling out of notebooks, its gestures everywhere
in middle age, the river whose bends
turn back to life from a specially calculated
distance. And when you have said what you will
of what is looked-for, you have said it above all
silently. Because the looked-for life is airy
and green, blowing away, or growing
up, its gestures fed to atoms, its workings very
nearly free, if never wholly freed, but passing truly by
in the tactful light of freeing. Smalls
referred once to small items of clothing, especially
underwear! Approaching the looked-for is like
being almost bared, shepherding the flock that used to
wander here, once, or before, or back when you remember
them, the sheep both soft and coarse, lost and nearly
found, what you looked for and called to,
smaller always for being remembered, here in the imposing
shadow of a mountain
whose ridge appears as the sun appears, appears
or disappears, as if all of earth
were wearing roses.

Analogue

A proverb comes in in the eleventh inning.
An orange is sectioned and shared in bed.
Water or sun has spotted the jacket
of yet another French philosopher.

I agree that patience is bitter
but its fruit is sweet. Look how far
the autumn shadblow went
with various gestures on your sheers,
how most clocks were wound by hand
for a reasonable,
or very long time.

Analogue

for Roy Wright

I was low, so I searched for your pencil drawing
of the sweet chestnut fruit—the infinitely spiky
female cupule—to think

what monkish discipline
makes a drawing so taxing and soft.
As rays bear with the sun, as each spoke

holds with the wheel,
you seem to have suffered the chestnut
as the shy host might a desired guest.

As Mica Means Crumb, and Galaxy, Milk

> *Cautro cosas tiene el hombre*
> *que no sirven en la mar:*
> *ancla, gobernalle, y remos,*
> *y miedo de naufragar.*
> —Antonio Machado

> *Perform no operation until all has become water.*
> —alchemical motto

I start with matter. Daylight's grain,
slag, scrap, and litter: core cuttings of fall, apples
mashed, dark drawer envelopes gathering seed.
Wherever nothing happens to the sand,

where it can settle
in the absence of vibration, it appears disposed
to pattern, as if the resined bow
were getting from the rim

a transposition, or deposition—the streaming of a mare
in gallop against the wind. Sleep, says a body,
but the ear stays on
for balance, knowing earth is both a handful and

a home. Sleep, and light is like a thing
put out at the prow. Sweeter now for being out.
Goodnight to daylight grain and seed. Sleep, says body,
but the ear is up, awake, at work,

to guide a dreamer's outstretched hand,
to reach and not to fall, to feel the lichened stones
are named with names of sailors, to measure lichen's
perfect crawl, the protracted troth

of alga-fungus,
slow and glowing as ever.
And you who are arrived at
just as slowly, what provisions have you brought

for dreaming, what's to be rationed
in the dark, in what economy of strokes and stars?
As mica means crumb, and galaxy, milk. As every cell aspires
to the whole of the memory. A ferry comes back

without a name. A fall crossing, a summer one.
Sometimes a spring light
bare as eggs
would spread on the Atlantic.

And *Orient Point*
comes back. And direction, like a rake,
rakes the pebbles backward from the shore,
each radiant gray and pink a minor piece

of the dragging glass of waves.
The sequence of romance is like this, a daylight series
of unduplicated exchange. A scarf-red item
dragged through dream. Or every

shedding yellow ever hanging at the prow.
Maybe there are breaks in the series. Things we coveted
above the rest.
Because a wooden boat held gleaming fish

in flowering lantern. Because this is a feeling
that might be loved to distraction.
Say that light was there
to give away. To be put out. As kinglet, gannet,

swallow and grebe, as petrel and pelican
give a skimming weight
to water's mapless dreaming.
As spring is part of dreams and part of winter.

As she makes the day-world cold, as she keeps its granite
crashed upon, and pocked, as spring has made her living
in a welling stream, in shell and clay,
brass and wood, in brass and wood and skin

and wind, icy and free, a discipline
tacked to light,
the curious mirror, in sharing and undoing, in marking
her momentum with retreat. As a handspan

has measured a horse, as outspread arms
compose a fathom, the riverbottom
seen is also leafmeal.
Not dark, but dormant gold, a torch

on the stone
of a narrow stairwell. Lake or river, body or body,
the instruments are only sylvan.
As first snow falls,

as the red-naped flicker chisels firs.
Hades fills his well with naked light.
Luminescence is the adaptation
for kissing

the sun good-bye. There's an old dog
in that dark, a frilled shark, a living fossil
in the depths of earthbound water.
For what is lower

than engraved, who is for these regions of the dream
soul alone will find compatible—black tracts
of magnetic spherules, frangible grains
of ravishing stars, loosest

aims of clayey matter, finest bits of cooled volcanic rock,
once ledged, once sifted down, oxides of iron
and manganese, earth in total catalogue
without sufficient light to read.

Autumn

Autumn was too close to solemn.

The silent *n*,
too understated for the season.
When a metallic feeling bit the air, Americans called it *fall*.

Let down
the dusk-blue grapes.
Let out the scope of chapters.

Cerebral

You may have some idea of who she was,
having seen her at her folding task.
Though she had not been domesticated
on her own terms, she could sometimes imagine
no other way than here,
hard by the bones of a house
whose thresholds invited her to be punctilious,
or thin, whose hours reached above her
like a beached nave. Mild, is how she'd sound
if she spoke to you, the same as how you'd sound
if you spoke to her. As a creek grows silver
even where it dims, the hallway is a careful place
for having words. Into whose long throat
she'll snap the laundered cloth,
taut as a sail in its feast of air, to set
a nightly table
or make the weekly bed.

Chair

The chair is a gesture. Of all
the ranging motions, there are two hands always
pulling the chair out, or one hand saying, Sit down,
it's free. Now its wood shines with absence.
Now it hardens to oak. Of all the wearing evenings
and mornings, the chair, unlike
a boat, is never named. Years pass and the chair goes by
in duplicate, profligate, a map of lowered anchors
printed so small they look like stars.

Coccolithic

after Elisabeth Vellacott's "Man Warming His Foot" (1971)

Your clouds appear to know the tumbled stones,
the blue and purple-brown of mussel shells,
how soon a falling cry

describes the redirection of the tide.
I think it must be cold as autumn in Britain.
There's nowhere to sit or have a glass.

Your door stays open to the day;
the room is aired with inexplicit light.
Outside a gull is orange against the chalk.

The Downs,
those cliffs, are lit
or blurred an even darker rose.

Who will move away, or who is moving in
isn't the watercolor's matter.
Back then

it was either him or him: a tall man
in gray socks, one foot planted on the floor,
one foot warming at the fire.

Coincidence

When everything broken is broken,
and everything dead is dead...
—Robert Hass, "Faint Music"

When the Devil you do know is inappreciably different
from the one you don't.

When the notch cut in the mourning circle whistles.
When you are very busy procrastinating

for the rest of your life. When the many hundred
blackbird updraft happens.

If, alphabetically, a bead falls somewhere
between a beach and a bear.

That I want to have an abacus
and don't pretend to know how an abacus works.

When a writer is quoting a writer
who says *Fantasy hesitates.* Like the hundred

black birds pecking
cold grass

did not hesitate to rise
at once from feeding. How it was fantasy,

not for the strong, concurrent uprush of wings,
but for the unison

hitch above the branches, a quieting pause
where flight had been, the lighting down

of passerine, their hesitation turning
fullness to precision.

Like breathing in the vicinity
of soot.

Like breathing in the vicinity—
between some or another earlier point in time

between some or another person speaking
your name. For two things

to coincide they might have had the option
not to. Good-bye for the present;

see you later.
As if I could learn to use an abacus properly.

There are things I will never learn
people I will never meet.

We say
gives rise to

as though to map time
topographically,

by touch, arousingly. How flat the a-
causal picture

where things just are; where nothing gives rise

to anything else. When
on the other hand

something not coinciding in time
does coincide in space—

Lo!
Lo!

—you can still call out
the old time

        syllable of astonishment,
the mutual

        light of symmetry, still face each other
kindly in the circumstance, in the softly integral turn

        a humanly hesitating
fantasy might have,

        the chorus conscience breaking from the poem,
backing out with wonted grace, bending as grass to weather,

        light
to dark, right here, right

        away, right where the running together of circumstances
without apparent causal connection

is. Listen,
        you could cut the word later
                out of idolater. You could find the word worshipper

in the earliest sense of later.
        It is not unlike a salary, a salting of cause
            with effect,

as a hook crosses
        the fish's path
            by bending that cross to a question.

Who can resist dragging a finger
        where fragrant
            sawdust settles, the lure of writing something

in something made of something else?

Color Wheel

Of the three
comings of the Lord, Bernard of Clairvaux called two
visible,
one, invisible

Jesus in the manger
was visible as dry straw on spun wool
as livestock's
patient breathing

Jesus of the Parousia should be visible as cochineal...

but green,
glassy as a sleeping midden, the other coming
is the hidden one:

home-like, liminal, made of whoosh
and wood, the wreath hung up

in plain sight, juniper-blue
as gin

Comedy

You've been given your coat, sewn with a coda.
Late for morning, early for evening, the generalities are coming down
in laxly sundered specks. What little magic might spread over us
is here. A sniff, a blink, a slow indexical trail
telling across the hall table, those coming, those going,
the dry, tickling, stuffy taste, a close-to-weightless
song of matter layering itself to rest, the same,
the sorry, the everywhere falling light and steady, heavy
and delayed, why, you'll kiss the very picture of it,
face and glass amassing days of it, motes and motes,
loose as you please, dry as a sifting snowfall
never made of water. But soft.
Cut from the same cloth. Of a body with. I think
we're near, we're almost there. But see how much this stuff
is like our leaving out all thought of us. Only touch
the sleeve, the seam. Dander, pollen, daydream.
It's good, the dream, I think. I think
it has to be.

Compounding Pharmacy

The stowaway   keeps quiet.

An undercroft   had better be what you hope it is.

A timepiece grows   more feathers underground.

A windfall is an apple   wise to attachment.

Disquiet adopted   a whetstone's grit.

Correctly

Seferis asks
what a flame can remember,
not to start a list like *woman, table, evening, spoon*—
but to think through the narrowing allowances.
Remembering too little, the flame goes out.
Remembering too much, the flame goes out.
Such that remembering is as carefully
measured as
the cordial kiss, or morbid rattle.
Because why remember at all, if not correctly,
the layering way that fire exhumes,
the secret translating spectacle
of Our Lady burning, blue song
of the peahen here, heavy-lidded Juno
of the genius woman over there, unbegun
and everlasting, clear as memory ever
was, her motives tied
to coruscation, unhooking the light
and bidding it run, her river
singing to the star of morning?
What else can a flame remember?
A knocking, a handshake, its moon,
dandelion sylphs and sky-walkers,
souls appointed to wing, sun-dappled tops
of woodland mayapple, breezy shining
of the deep-eyed dogwood, an extinguished
campfire of reasons.
This morning's crewelwork of birdsong—
would you, would you, would you—
Bare fluttering sound
of the plant
beside you
would I would I would I

Custody of the Eyes

Should this mean adding the slow returns
in shadowed columns, currying to a glow the dappled
horse of her alone in winter stall, should winter stall
be gold with summer-windrowed hay, hay she'd aired
and cured, the sweeter for bedding and feeding.
Could she be leaning backward after faith, leaner for
the habit of not looking, promised to the long, dry
braid of disincentive with incentive. It takes
a kind of will. And then some time apart. Abashed,
crushed in—in earshot, still, of holding dear.
Her grazing won't have asked to see.
Will have stood beyond velleity, the pollen path
of lightest wishing, the fair, but faintest blues
of nothing almost carried out.

"Diabolic Clouds Over Everything"

—*Ruskin,* "The Storm Cloud of the 19th-Century"

Then a scotched bird will drop in another fire of particulars.
Then another will fall.

No one will draw in the future. Soon we will stop
having to ask,

What must the future hold? The dismemberment of being
subject to time

is only, at bottom, temporary. As you'll know
if you held

a bird in your palm. For the love of God,
or otherwise.

Do No Harm

As if the bird were not in one room,
but many, and making the sound of many seabirds
pinning dunes to blue and vibrant yards of wind.
That sanding down

was why,
was surely what I felt the credo
was: no mean or desperate motion, no graceless
tangling in the rafters, but light as fire to an open flue,
the relic beehive feathering up to ashes in the draft. This was where
I told myself to live. And pressed my life to going over
everything I did.

Eunomia

Are you at home.
And where is a conscious moment
for the one tree leaning at the sky.
For apple trees.
And where is that. Are you
a conscious moment. A woken tact
and practice. The furred sound of purple hyssop
bowed over by bees. Is it simple as a pattern
you could mind and marry. Alone with incensed
rooms, sea-water woods. Are you at home
in windows. In the sapphire life
of particles. What is the age at which
it comes to you—a pack
of last beech leaves, deep and airy
gold, whole orders whizzing to the ground?
There is a home some ways from home.
Yesterday is carried thin as a note.
Much as a letter once traveled the dark,
just out ahead
of the sleeping receiver.

Gloriana

*Do not tell secrets to those whose faith and silence you
have not already tested.*
—Elizabeth I

As water, were it not for gravity's leveling
pull, should be, of its own will, spherical,
her sovereignty shouldn't soften for a
second. This handmade moon, these stars,
this wired and starchy ruff around her—no
not for a second should these be softened.

Housework

A deer that falls
no longer scatters. A bee

is filling
in the ribs. The

leaves?
Become the apron's detail work.

Her eyesight
changes in the woods.

Idle

You had sometimes had the look
of a dark-eyed junco. I had liked it when you would find me
something out of the way and old, how you put things to me
as simple questions, made your lowliest actions
fair and esoteric, but never with affectation,
and never to the point of stalling.
Few things of a human nature
enchant you anymore. It's true forbearance
doesn't happen by itself. The piano would nurse
a judder for days, but only when it wasn't played.
Your music had always had this way of falling off.
Decay was something you could really savor, falling
and falling quiet. You'd always liked
fall's cider taste,
if not completely the season.

Insofar

                    as you are
forewarned they say you are
forearmed. I'd like
to remember what a warning is. How it slips
through caution into notice.
How it slips
through creation
as creation's second condition. One
centimeter in a hundred days.
The health of a nail
is evident
in the moon-shaped
matrix of cells where some
have said
a human's fate begins.
A nail moves out
from under its cuticle.
I see what is noticed
is only
sometimes what is known. Little moons,
lunulae, I try to remember
what the remotest
human was.

Insofar

                    as it is only the ground moving,
you have seen that before.
And because there is the compulsion
to look up close
at that which you are given to see
more often from afar,
you will go to have a closer look
at the bird your cat has killed
and put aside:
a stiff, red-chested robin.
Blood has stopped supplying
his eyes. His corneas have clouded
over, whiter, you think,
than milk,
an opacity so shot with privacy
you must drop your pretension to
whatever it was
you thought you were doing,
such as thinking to minister,
such as thinking of ministry
as a thing within
your power to confer.
Then a plane you can't see passes
your life diagonally, raking light above
the clouds, and you are turned
from your attentions
to the bird,
or was it singular: turned
from paying attention?

Insofar

        as the pieces move
over some period of time,
insofar as quartz splits, and the moon half appears
to padlock the tide, so long as wet sand is skirted
by itching mist and flies, what goes before
grows wildly antecedent. Flecks
of volcanic glass, freshening grains
of skeleton and shell. There is no blood,
but a water vascular system
straining oceans through a sieve, a five-point,
radial symmetry, eyes at the end of their arms,
no color-detecting cones, no lenses
to focus light. Clouds have built
their shadows in the troughs. Whoever sees
the shining detours of the stars
sees them pose and move the question
back to sea: what is mine
to keep, or miss?
I know a starfish is not a fish.

Insofar

        as the golden larch grows out another spring,
insofar as the needles look gold or copper

with the close of the growing season—and fall
like the milk teeth of a mammal, deciduous,

insofar as deciduous is what falls down or off, really
what is *cut* off, insofar as a thing can be cut off

from its other, extraneous, as in the making
of decisions, as in the feeling of *this* being severed

from an adjacent feeling for *that*, as if these feelings
had not a common vertex and a common side,

insofar as the tree you have in mind is both
coniferous and deciduous, could it not be turning

a color darkly adjacent to green, insofar as
coniferous is cone-bearing but not also evergreen

in every case, insofar as a golden larch is real,
and real is then the feeling of those cones

shaped like small artichokes, in a mast season,
when they boss the golden larch like pieces

of ornamental carving covering the point
where the ribs in a vault or ceiling cross,

insofar as architecture might be analogous
to arboriculture, or until a wind or creature

should detach a cone, which will easily detach,
insofar as it is a golden, and not a true larch,

and once detached, will cast its long-winged seeds
to life, insofar as life is there to catch them, to heave

and bury them, insofar as actions are decisions
as to what is or is not continuous.

Liquidity

Though I have never stopped in Sandusky
I know what the word remembers of the Wyandot people:

cold water.

Where does the time go.
Like other people, I occasionally say this aloud.

I think we should be clear as we can
as to where the time goes.

Yesterday afternoon, sunlight stood
just one tree out

from the woods. I wish for things
in addition to water

to take on
the shimmer of water.

Monotonic

The same being apparently no longer
the same, but still. Here are the apples
cutting into stars, the cedar-scented wool
of late, or failed apology, the emptied
trees and sliver moons, the increasingly
ubiquitous air of the sad coffee shop
with its tender painting of a breaching
whale. They say the sign of a syncopated
body is blood pressure plummeting,
strong beats where you couldn't want
them, weak ones where you would.
Ah, Sunflower. Green or mythic face
of a rounded self. Your commonest dawn
is like the wispy tops of sweetening
carrots. Or so I have come to think of
seed. To love what holds its course
and has its way, the comparative
adverb, *oftener*, the moldy afterlife
of leaves, the surgically
minor key
of a former century's waltz.

Mutual of Omaha's *Wild Kingdom*

As the legs of a wild animal slow and falter,
as the addled creature falls in a rare
discoordination of joints, so he was
tranquilized: anesthetic chemicals entered
his heart by way of a ballistic hypodermic
needle feathered at one end, a man-made
dart, quiet as an apple-turning breeze. Now
there is the one who is out cold in our
televisions. And there is the one who was
caught, examined, and returned to the wild.
Sunlight pauses on their auburn heads. A
mother watches from her blue shadows. As
a foal fishes for its legs, as a sleeper shakes
off remnant threads of strong dreaming.
Sunlight pauses with the trees. A flamingo
lifts to a straight, dry flame.

Noon

I will give you a glass of water. Tell me a story of thirst.
Once magnolias

were rampant, lush as knifed-scraped oysters
in Madison Square Park. *Glissant, nowed, couchant,*

salient.
There was no honey like a honey yet to be had.

The sunsets darkened like cooked sugar.
Connection buzzed the surfaces.

The ferries went back and forth. Watery Manhattan
held its breath. When Romans

invented the lustrum, it was the sacrifice
that purifies.

The same people who went out believing
noon is the hour thickest with ghosts.

Openly

Who isn't a little tired of being social
when it takes so much surveillance from every side.
You don't stop being hard on other people,
but the love you do dispense is spiral,
and wildly celibate.

Wedded to the glisten of a moving wave,
your creature in the sand, her sensible retraction
into shell, the perfect opalescence
of her seam—there's nothing there
but caving daylight.

Or later, the philosophical sketch of shell,
a drawing like the bees waxed wooden
turn of banister.

That shell was like a virtue
showing up in the sand, as strangely,
distantly violate. Like the v in violate, the v
in violence, it wedges somewhere
unforgivably in your mind, the pot coming
to a rapid boil, the generalizing sting of vinegar,
a spotted shell on the window sill,
striped towels flapping on the line.

Some had called it *cleaning*,
not *killing*. Some said *memento*
when later holding up the shell.

Platform

There is a surface from which to step on or off a train

The specific feeling of shoes with extra thick soles

There is a book Narcissus left us like a thirst for reading

How many will fit its silhouette

How will it look like faces

Since when are so many clicking sounds human

What is a profit in our image

What writing is on the wall and moving

This is not a natural sign above a small canoe

still going across a lake?

Poem

It sounds heavy,
to *bear* resemblance, but you have a way of carrying it off,
bearing it lightly as you do,
light as the sword lilies you keep at your side
clipped from the skyline of your cutting garden.

It's how you stand in line to say good-bye.
It's how your hands lift up as you give them away.

You talk like someone I used to know.
More starkly, now, than I remember.

If this bears resemblance to your voice
it's as the ideogram stands for the moon,
or as the brush is ducked in ink,
and wiped at the mouth of the pot.

Still abroad?
A solidus in your pocket?
I have something for you. But my girl,
you have got to come home.

Polygraph

for until the cord be broken the bird cannot fly…
—Saint John of the Cross

It was bird language gone just enough awry
to turn each bird a raptor in its heart of hearts.
It was fiendish and convincing as the birds in *The Birds*.
It was the *poly-* in polygraph,
a pen strapped to one and every fluctuation
a wingless body could supply. It wasn't like telling
a practiced story; the device was roped
to the effects of voice. *Swear it.*
I swear. The shape of a dead parrot
is polygon. Its decomposing underside is yellow-
green. *Detection is, or ought to be, an exact science.*
So said Sherlock Holmes, who solved one crime
by noticing the depths to which parsley sinks in butter.
We know in our bones it's true. Detection's a well
of mossy sensation. It's just as the poet wrote.
A poem should end like a rope.

Practical Transparency

Out of the communal bowl of abstractions
I picked transparency. The knife struck carefully
against the glass—I gathered it signaled a toast,
or time for the wedded couple to kiss.
Transparency grew audible as wine.
It was a near thaw that made a circumference
in the river, that precarious circle of ice. What thaws,
softens, but can conserve and edge, a thinness
keeping round in rising, passing water.
Spring was just beginning in the Flathead Valley.
It magnified our walk, the contacts of stone
and fallen matter. Insofar as transparency
is real, it was fairly taking place, an insulation
you could speak and look through.
Where truth was turning the wheel of its hawk,
hunting purely with what she sensed,
I was hoping to know solemnity
in the very flight of surroundings.
A photograph is one thing. A window,
another. And another, just transpiring.
Fire was coming in variable quantities,
blue, mesmeric, high, quiet. I saw the sawing
of light into color could be casual,
or covenant. The sometimes feather-blue
of a pencil tip grew increasingly sharp, its property,
crystalline and allotropic, its pressure,
conditionally responsible.
In the picture you gave me,
the river was holding itself up.
In that small lens of self-inspection,
it trembled with holding still. Duomo,
Diablo, when was my conscience nearly
so clear? Here is the sound
before the toast. Say something
good and real.

Quetzalcoatl

That my soul companion is a dog

That we are cremated together

That my twin has the narrow face of a hound

That the evening star is the sun's sole companion

That the morning star is the sun's sole companion

That the sun dies-and-rises as a matter of course

That the sun is asymmetrical as an eye

That dogs have the way to the Land of the Dead by heart

That the Land of the Dead leaves bones in the care of jewels

That jewels are the filing system

That jade is the coolest jewel

That humankind was compounded by walking upright

That the chill between compounds is spidered with stars

That walking upright creates companions

That the Lord of the dead is known for such wiliness

That owls perch upon the Lord's decisions

That red feathers come from eating plants

That orange feathers come from eating plants

That the red and yellow and orange beard you are growing is made of feathers

That bones are postures on loan

That debt is never linear

That you may take what you want from the Lord of the Dead

That his fame extends from the loaning of bones

That every loan is attached to an *if*

If you are asked to play a conch that has no holes

If a conch shell in the Land of the Dead is unbreathable

If you are as likely to get music from stone

That my strangest companion is my twin

That we are cremated together in the space of fire

That music must have its way

That worms are making holes for all of time

That bees have the rhythm of desire

That humming can only work off surface

That every loan is attached to an *if*

If this is a material cycle

If earth is not to be passed through easily

If learning is learning

If there is a god of wind and learning

And that serpent can be feathered and faced

And an air is a song but also a manner

And a cross section is seeing everything

where everything means excepting the whole

Radical Empiricism

This morning your letter arrives
as letters used to: folded twice

to a triptych, smudged where your palm
followed the pen too quickly. Slew grass—

did I know it?—grows high enough
horse and rider might go unnoticed

riding through it, buried from sight
in a meadow of it

Radius

...around every circle another can be drawn
—Emerson, "Circles"

You pointed out a woodenness, coaxed its rose
to wandering, made every door real with refusal, sly
with admission. I have seen you lighting on the landscaped

mirror. Your oil
looks functional down to the burning pond.
There's a murmur, a purl, to your single-most discipline.

You burden like a mess I haven't finished making. Like starlings
you are drawing
all the starlings from the sky.

Rappelling

There came a time when people refused to start a sentence with it. There were some who kept its custom, for whom going to sleep was still a form of secular confession. Because— Because— Eyes closed, mouths open, they fed it out like rope to the bottom of the pitch-dark   sentences, nightly descending on the strength of its unknown direction. And only when they felt reasonably assured they had gotten to the bottom of something, only then would they tilt their faces to the squid of the sky, its partially reasonable stars. Then and only then would they yell back up—*Drop the rope!* But fixed at a higher point, whatever tree saw to it that the rope was secure in these instances knew it had no means of untying the rope, no words with which to say so. And the rappeller had anyway dropped below a listenable distance, had already found another rope, and on the strength of another tree, had already begun a next descent.

Selkie

Seal-stone.
Not one to seal a spirit's letter,

but sea-gray, and greasy.
Sedentary,

though sometimes quickened.
Gray to calendula's orange-yellow.

As animated when wet
as ever evolution was.

Lucky stone, however
stranded in the woods.

Shellycoat

The child found the bridge above the river.
Fog took its net of water to their face.

Sky was a circuitous idiom. Willow was a new school
of reflection. From Stars, they learned to sew.

They sewed a coat that fell to their ankles.
It took them years but they wore it.

It took them years.
And if at night they wandered—whispered

and shimmered with shells—if haunting was all
a moon would give them to do, they'd make each

walker strain to listen, sway off course,
and wander with them.

Shodo

What is habit
to the river. The hand-wiped mirror
only silvers over with steam. Last night's wood
is white where it burned, and black. Red is the lifeline color
for a shaman's tethering mitten. As you must return to something,
as far as you know. As a mitten chooses
where a hand is halved.
As the stiff heart wants slackening. As spring appears
in radical snowdrops when recalled, as no one
never minded earth, as some balance is struck asymmetrically,
as the brush keeps pace with horses, trees,
gratitude, honor, grace.

So Far Out

Light lipped off the mirror's leafy border.
The flower arrangement fell apart.
The dog was chewing a rosary
with a patience too gentle to mind.
The careful bubble of the spirit level
split and split. Could the rose
say just some of what the summer
lightning said. *Who doesn't fail.*
Who doesn't fail at this.
I dreamed, I woke, I rose.
The leaves were falling
faster in my mind.
At dawn, a bliss of silver
on my neighbor's pond.

Suncatcher

Why all this time, the sun is a stable star, a gift, a given.
Why the glassmaker chose a thing
as tired as an angel.

Why the disc,
hanging off a purple ribbon, is a core sample of passing time,
a telescope folded in, a lone eye looking from the kitchen
to the distant styles of burial grounds, shearing
shelves of ice, blues more terribly immediate
for having fallen nearly out of form.

Why a circle is androgynous.
Why time runs hot and cold. When to fill the bath. Why trees fill in.
There's *chronos* to pin the sun to sequence, and *kairos* to catch
the sun off guard.

As at times a liquid glint will coat the disc
in its habit of spinning slowly sideways, as if a match
could burn in water, quickly found, or barely dreamed, a blue
outdoing blue, in the disc's phenomenal turn,
in the strangely collective life of fire, fire whose hottest silver
is marine, in the schooling shimmer of where things go, the loose
but unanimous pivot
of the bound,
if sudden-minded shoal.

Taliesin

Light slings us together as shadows

We are goshawk spiral and scampering vole

We are most slippery otter and most beautiful trout

To all outward appearances I had aimed to disappear—to be a life

absorbed by life: corn in so much barn-dark corn, water as seen

through water—

but there is a mother I remember

more than once, a tufted hen that swallowed me

—a witch that would ever

pick me out

The Depletions

My thoughts are all a case of knives.
—George Herbert

In the middle of the night I find myself in a thematic seminar. Tables
have been pushed together into a square "O" so that no one's facing

another person's back. Where the young seminarians sit in the middle
of the night, I begin to see what the theme is. It's like a thin path

of starlight threading through a chorus that hasn't begun to sing. And
just at the end of this thread, someone or other will solo. *Silence is scarce.*

Silence is depleted. It's hard to say what silence is. I like the seminarians.
By this time they have taught me their spirit animals. They are scientific

and kind. They would measure silence carefully, find it a quantity,
an economics, some new consideration of home that won't be so

blurry as ours. And though I am listening with great interest, and though
I envy them their disciplines—*silence is scarce, silence is depleted*—

their measures of silence elude me. The denominator eludes me. The stars
are getting in the way of math. The stars are a static interference I cannot clear—

a bright and enticing tangle of qualia and connotation. Depletion had always
sounded clean, like pleats, what they call *knife pleats* on skirts or kilts.

Depletion had appeared to have a clean edge, unlike other ideas of removal
and reversal. But where pleats root in folding, depletion roots in full space,

the plenum, to remove from or reverse from which is the endless work
of depletion. But how to imagine this as quantity? Some of the seminarians

will be future doctors. Have they learned that depletion therapy was once
the measure doctors undertook with patients, bleeding them back

to an imagined balance of humors? That just like that a paradigm can colonize
the mind until its told, *Enough, you're doing harm?* Measures are being taken today

future doctors will have to decry. If silence has a somewhere entirety,
a faraway plenum played out here as a revolving material-imaginal, flickered

as a wheel, as a fullness in the analogical sense that you are, or I am open
to running out of time, then I imagine silence might also be finished

being depleted, done with lancets and fleams and blood-thirsty bowls.
In the middle of the night I see a body suffering. I see a body

has always its pivots of time and courses of travel, its several reasons
fastened to departure. In the stars a bow draws taut, and tauter.

In the morning, I will not pray to received forms at the last minute.
I have regularly prayed to the old circulations of love and reason:

sweetness, sourness, bile, forests of lightly disturbed quiet. I will pray to
the reindeer gods secreting a knife-edge ambivalence. Back to the wooden

chair, feet to the wooden floor, I know that this is why I must adjust
my thinking to a humorous or sinking thought. A bow draws taut,

and tauter. In the sour sweetness of winter apples I've a wakening sense
of measure, in truth, it's another session, as when reason can be taught

to come out, made to sit down with reflection, reflection having had, and
with good reason survived, its latest falling out with window, mirror, water.

"The Hour Has Come to Remember the Dead"

—Anna Akhmatova

Whoever heard the wind strike five,
Or the clock, rip a cricket from the grass

Whoever saw stars shine into locked cells
For whomever the dove cooes in the distance

And the snow
Prepares the flower

The idle afternoon of a candlestick
A bright day and a deserted house

Your premonition coming true,
Drawing a calm, vertical line

To the evening
It waits to bring to light

The Kiss

Snowflakes holding their corners
just above a thaw, a kelp-like
shine of ivy over the library's
donated walls.

A radio turning
white with static, a sightline cut off
by the downward slope
of a parking garage.

What descends
with me: two persons running down a path
in dark parkas.
Two hoods leaning in.

A quick
and quickening impulse
in wet snow
and high wind.

The Path Back Barely Findable

If it rains, brother,
it rains, if losing your place in reading when called to look up,
notice what is also there for us, hard buds at the glass
where the branches are hurled, daylight sped
toward nothing apparent.

We have studied for years
what loyalty is, but look how thrown,
if loyal, the senses are. Should a calling awaken me
or you, should we sleep right through the middle of it.
If woods are where their calling is. Should a deer stand also
in the field, subject to frost, and time, and distance,
should grace stand there also
with nothing to do.

The Prefecture

It was impossible to picture *mouth* and *source* at once:
locating the one displaced the other. Then word arrived

of a nearby gorge.
Water grew audible as a way through rock.

Then the field of vision went to seed.
A child fell,

like cooling mist, on its own corresponding
grownup face. Who knew how long

we were stopping there.
"There" was nothing but pounding water.

You were the first to motion us forward.
To picture the temple

we'd left behind. How the pulled-
back beam would be striking the bronze,

how rain would have curtained,
and shimmered the sound.

Thoughts Before Whittling

for Arden

When a block of wood
falls into your hands,
angle the knife away,
skim the wood as you would milk.
Listening for what to do next is this
transparent, the bones of the ear,
this exactingly small.
As you were
will be the command
restoring you to love.
You will not
pretend to forget
what is hard
and innermost here.
Years ago,
you were gifted a tea set
that made no sense.
So miniature the cups,
the pot, the creamer—
any attempt at ceremony
could only overrun them.
Do not deceive me,
soul,
and I will no more
pour you away.

Tidy

It would start out speaking
to the while or season
we think of as duration.

It would start out meaning
timely or opportune,
with an eye to the rising

and falling sea. Thus,
at Yuletide,
Oden was said to set

a Wild Hunt
across the winter sky.
I like being alone

in winter,
the stark apostles,
wind, snow, and stone.

I like what is
seasonal and real.
The Wild Hunt is made of stars.

Tithonos

What
else might I have been
had I the power to die? She nominates

all waking paths with light. Being wed
so far to dawn, there is no darkening
field on earth

this gift won't keep me from.

Unsound Supposition

Two wasp-stings in one day. The brown
and unaggressive paper-wasps had only just begun
the small umbel of their hive when your telescoping
ladder reached their height.
Acid for wasp venom, alkaline for bee. How deadly
sweet it is, a datum, how way beside the point,
but pointed nonetheless, these desirable
stings of quibbling, quarreling,
jockeying for the smallest powers.
I read that *Petty Dancers*
is an older name for Northern Lights.
A whale
had fur. A mouse was once
a budding whale. The evolutionary question is
why come out of the water.
We say lichen is fungus,
but alga, too, a cracked shield,
a case of mutualism we can agree is pretty cool.
In a human light, the filling of summer hours
swings between petty and magnanimous,
between dampened
drums of thunder, sheets of rain you eyed
from the front window, numbering the obligations
to a house.
Water makes these curious lines. I'm right,
you're wrong. You're wrong, I'm right.
Unsound supposition, that the overflow
was caused by leaves.

Vital Materiality

for JC

A shop clerk wraps a cage in nineteenth century newspaper, concealing the nature of the purchase, the gift of a singing goldfinch. I picture bright yellow, but Hardy would have had in mind the European kind: chestnut brown, red-masked, black-crowned, gold only in the bars jagging across his coal-black wings. The same week I come to the end of the novel I laugh at your complaint: is there no theory of the numinous *that isn't completely bloody mystical?* Henchard had intended for his daughter the reparative gift of a living bird. But wrapped in so much news, the cage is discovered by no one inside the novel in time to rescue its bird from a slowly imagined starvation.

When My Sister Poets Leave

When my sister poets leave,
gasses are prickling breakfast water
no one has cleared from the table.
Staying takes up a lazy motion, whatever scope
the anchor's chain allows. When my sister
poets leave, June's past, *fossilized*
is an earthy word with spiritual flavor.
I wave until I go inside. Where long orange light
seeds the paperweight sphere,
a blown glass ball
near the window's catch
comparing the woods to fire.

Where Are the Days of Tobias

The fresco cracks cooperatively over time. Not to give a secret away
but gradually to break off keeping it. In the sky you make birds
like this, one wing longer than the other, an asymmetrical v
wedged against wind, one stroke longer than another,
never the bodies turned the same direction, each finding
its own angle, and one, in the distance,
a dot. These are the Deadly Birds of the Soul
Rilke was forced to call *terrifying.*
Migratory, weighing no more than a pencil.
Because every flying thing is passionate, and every flight
a posture torn from stone.
There was a time it was a theme
parents would pay an artist to realize—the face of a beloved son,
a Luca or Piero, painted onto the shoulders of Tobias,
painted into the company of Raphael. You tell yourselves
and your quiet house
no harm will come to the boy
as he goes out. A guardian, though, is not a guard. To keep safe
is subtly different from confining. Radiance can strategically
direct itself to seem like us, ready, as it were, to walk.
As a mirror goes through the appearance of requiring
subsistence, goes through the motions of a meal
whose food appears to be food.
Radiance, we know, is never quite as warm as light.
Who has not tasted the silver in sea mist?
Whosoever they are, angels are the first to surface there.
You know a guardian by the silver of a river-crossing,
of a father's filmy eyes, in gall, heart, fire,
and mostly smoke. In smoke and mostly mirror.
As, wedged between forward and backward being,
rehashing and planning ahead, presence will be specked again
with being erased, a reusable writing surface
calling down to the life without rest, the self-propelled
surveillances of sharks.

Zephyrus in Four Corners

I.

Where the face of this god is filling up
the redbud flowers at its bark
the grasses dream of lying down

II.

In whose flipped leaves and rattled fruits
is the paint for this god still votive blue?

III.

All it took to allay the sun:
his angled return to immediate trees.

IV.

When its red broke down to copper ovals,
was the pond as winded
as I was?

Acknowledgments

The American Journal of Poetry: "Color Wheel"

Antioch Review: "Tidy"

Basalt: "Shodo," "Shellycoat"

Bennington Review: "'The Hour Has Come to Remember the Dead'," "The Kiss"

Birmingham Poetry Review: "Liquidity"

concīs: "Autumn"

Conjunctions: "As Mica Means Crumb, and Galaxy, Milk"

Dusie: "The Prefecture" (as "Chapter 25")

Harvard Review Online: "Suncatcher"

The Hampden-Sidney Poetry Review: "Insofar," "Poem," "Rappelling"

Image: "Custody of the Eyes"

Interim: "Practical Transparency"

likestarlings: "Alibi"

Linebreak: "The Path Back Barely Findable"

Magma: "Insofar," "'Diabolic Clouds Over Everything'"

Mantis: "Monotonic," "Noon," "Polygraph"

Meniscus: "Thoughts Before Whittling"

Meridian: "Quetzalcoatl"

Minerva Rising: "Vital Materiality"

New England Review: "Insofar"

new sinews: "Chair," "Compounding Pharmacy," "Do No Harm,"
        "Unsound Supposition"

Ocean State Review: "Correctly"

Phoebe: "So Far Out"

Poetry: "Where Are the Days of Tobias"

Poetry Daily: "Insofar" (from *New England Review*)

Poetry Wales: "Radical Empiricism" (as "Faith"), "Taliesin"
        (as "Taliesin Speaks of Ceridwen")

Sycamore Review: "Insofar"

Talking River: "Radius"

Third Coast: "Mutual of Omaha's *Wild Kingdom*"

Transom: "Analogue," "Openly"

West Branch Wired: "Coincidence," "Comedy," "Eunomia," "Idle," "Platform"

The lines quoted on my dedication page are excerpted from Jeremy Hooker's poem, "As a Thousand Years," reprinted from the 2006 edition of *The Cut of the Light: Poems 1965-2005* with the permission of Enitharmon Press.

Lines from "What is the Language Using Us For?" by W.S. Graham are from New Collected Poems (Faber and Faber, 2004). Copyright © the estate of W.S. Graham, 2004. All rights reserved.

Thank you, Jeremy Hooker, for your poems and friendship. Thank you, Liz Meacham, and Lake Erie Institute friends, for strengthening paths of kinship and wisdom. Thank you, Meena Alexander, in memoriam, for selecting "The Depletions" for Poetry Society of America's 2018 Cecil Hemley Award. Thank you, Paula Bohince, for selecting "Housework" for PSA's 2019 Emily Dickinson Award. Thank you, Forrest Gander, for this honor of the Green Rose Prize. I am ever grateful for the love and support of my family, friends, and students.

photo by Ann Gridley

Sarah Gridley is an associate professor of English at Case Western Reserve University in Cleveland, Ohio. Her poetry collections include *Weather Eye Open* (University of California Press); *Green is the Orator* (University of California Press); and *Loom* (Omnidawn). She has a B.A. in English and American Literature from Harvard University, and an MFA in poetry from the University of Montana.

The Green Rose Prize

2019: Sarah Gridley
Insofar

2018: Lauren K. Alleyne
Honeyfish

2017: Doreen Gildroy
Trilogy

2016: Nadine Sabra Meyer
Chrysanthemum, Chrysanthemum

2015: Bruce Cohen
Imminent Disappearances, Impossible Numbers &
Panoramic X-Rays

2014: Kathleen Halme
My Multiverse

2013: Ralph Angel
Your Moon

2012: Jaswinder Bolina
Phantom Camera

2011: Corey Marks
The Radio Tree

2010: Seth Abramson
Northerners

2009: Malinda Markham
Having Cut the Sparrow's Heart

2008: Patty Seyburn
Hilarity

2007: Jon Pineda
The Translator's Diary

2006: Noah Eli Gordon
A Fiddle Pulled from the Throat of a Sparrow

2005: Joan Houlihan
The Mending Worm

2004: Hugh Seidman
Somebody Stand Up and Sing

2003: Christine Hume
Alaskaphrenia
Gretchen Mattox
Buddha Box

2002: Christopher Bursk
Ovid at Fifteen

2001: Ruth Ellen Kocher
When the Moon Knows You're Wandering

2000: Martha Rhodes
Perfect Disappearance